First Kiss

A Modern Romantic Story Set In A Small Village,
Including Intimate Moments Of Affection

*(A Comprehensive And Detailed Instruction On How To
Expertly Kiss A Girl For The First Time)*

Steve Chappell

"Fire!" he exclaimed.

Kayla felt her stomach churn. A seasoned rancher shuddered in terror at that one word.

"Do you have shovels?"

"Come on in, I got them!"

Kayla and her brother hopped into the pickup. "Where?"

"I believe it was near the fence line on the rear pasture. It was unclear to me which way it was coming from. From up near my home, I spotted it. Clint and Mike had already made their way there. Is the trailer necessary? Is there any stock available?

"No, all cattle are in the turn-out pens up here." While you were in Dallas last night, I asked the boys to bring them up. Before letting them go to graze, we must figure out how they leave. The east pasture is home to most horses, with the stables housing the remaining animals. You know what happens if it gets to the hog pens or the hen house.

The main ranch home had the hog pens, and the hen house was just out back. They were all in trouble if the fire spread that far.

Along the fence line, Gavin turned the pickup onto a horse trail. Salt Cedar Ranch was stretched out over five thousand acres, give or take an acre or two. Kayla and Gavin inherited the ranch when their parents died in a horrific car accident together. At the age of two,

Gavin was a cowpoke; by the time he was nine, he was a cowboy. He had no desire to be involved in the commercial aspect. Hard labor didn't bother him, but he was an outdoor man at heart. It would kill him to be cooped up behind a computer screen, on the phone, or worse, in meetings with people wearing suits. Although Gavin owned half of the ranch, Kayla managed its business side until it endangered their future; at this point, she sought his advice.

"What time did you return?" It was difficult, but she was trying not to bring up the black eye and the split lip.

"I arrived late yesterday evening. This morning, Mike and I were inspecting the fence breach when we noticed the fire.

By now, it has most likely been burning for at least 30 minutes.

"Have you given Wes a call?"

Yes, I did phone him. They were nearing the end of a task in the northern part of the town. They will require more than a minute to arrive at this location.

Wes Granger owned a private firm of rural responders. During the peak fire season, he maintained a crew of six smokejumpers on duty around the clock and a second aircraft carrying retardant. When Kayla took over the ranch, she insisted they required a service similar to his. Gavin was not persuaded. She felt sure he was reconsidering it now. She would hold off on saying, "I told you so," until the fire was out and everyone and everything was safe. They may then discuss his face in more detail.

"What is the estimated size of the fire?" she inquired.

"It was only about a hundred acres when I first saw it, but with this breeze, I think we'll be looking at twice that, at least by now."

After that, they traveled in quiet. Way out there, Kayla was racking her brains, figuring out how a fire might have started. No spark should have gone that far unless one of the electric fences went wild. Strange things had been happening on the ranch a lot lately. She held Tuck Stevenson, their new neighbor, responsible. In any case, Kayla had that theory. The only issue was that he was quite good at hiding his tracks, so Kayla had no evidence linking him to all the trouble.

As they approached the fire, Kayla noticed the heavy smoke beginning to appear and could also smell the charred grass. After stopping his truck on the side of the road, Gavin leaped out. She watched him effortlessly snap open the barbed wire between two fence posts with his bolt cutters. On the other side of the trail, two ranch horses were tied up; she figured those were the ones Mike and Clint had ridden out. Gavin leaped back in and drove the pickup off the path into the open grasslands. Not much would be harmed out here as long as they put out the fire soon. They would have difficulties if the wind changed and it began to burn down the slope toward the home, barn, and stables.

As they approached, Mike and Clint were visible, and the way the flames shot up behind them made them appear like a scene from Dante's Inferno. Now Kayla could hear its roar. There was a lot of cracking and crackling to go along with the sound, similar to what a wave does as it crashes into the rocks after breaking out of the water. Gavin pulled the pickup a good distance from the fire and in the opposite direction of its flames. They climbed out and retrieved the shovels from the vehicle's rear. Kayla had also taken along a couple of fire extinguishers, but it was a moot issue as soon as they got close enough to witness the monster's already enormous size.

Kayla let her gaze wander across the fire. It appeared the wall of flames went on forever, and the wind pushed it forward. Feeling completely powerless, she despised the elements. She took a deep breath and forced herself to get back into gear. She grabbed one of the shovels and went to join Mike and Clint as they dug frantically along the fire line. Taking up a place at the opposite end, Gavin coordinated with the others to try and dig a trench large enough to contain the fire until the smoke jumpers could reach it. After just a few minutes of work, Kayla's eyes were watering so much it felt like she was looking through a waterfall, and the smoke was entering her lungs through her open mouth and nose.

"Use this right here." Mike reached into his pocket for a handkerchief he gave her. Kayla covered her face with it, revealing only her eyes. Her eyes were hurting, and although it helped a little, her chest continued to hurt.

Above them, the fire held its head with pride, wreaking havoc and glaring at everything in its path, daring anyone to stand up to its incredible might. A slight change in the wind caused offensive smoke and ash to fall into their eyes and hair, devouring everything in its path. That served as a warning of what was to come. The wind ignited the fire, which also served as a catalyst, propelling it rapidly down the hill toward them. Kayla stood enthralled by it for a brief while, seemingly mesmerized by it.

At last, the magic shattered as Gavin grabbed Kayla's arm and said, "Dang it, Kayla, run!"

She bolted. It was already a hundred yards to Mike and Clint. Gavin stayed by her, and she heard the sound of the planes passing overhead as they ran. Thank God, reinforcements are on the way!

When they got to the pickup, they ran. Gavin observed the aircraft as they flew around the fire, descending with each passing flight. "Get in the truck; he's going to dump!"

Just as the bottom of the tiny aircraft opened up and a plume of what appeared to be orange foam shot out, the four of them climbed aboard. It seemed to enrage the flames at first, but it swept across the top. As though attempting to reach out into the sky and seize hold of the small plane, the flames shot upward. The pilot released another orange plume after freeing the aircraft from the monster's clutches. That one seemed to calm the fire down a little, and a few seconds later, the smoke jumpers were leaping out of the other plane, one by one, and the horizon was dotted with the colors of their billowing parachutes. Kayla grabbed her brother's arm as Gavin reached for his door doorknob.

"What are you doing?"

There appear to be just four of them. I'll lend a hand. Return the vehicle to the path and wait for us there. He managed to break free from his sister's hold, and as he opened the door, a plume of smoke swirled in from the wind. Clint and Mike got out together after Mike opened the door from his side.

Where do you go when trying to find the boy you want to kiss in the middle of a wild party? I look around the room I'm in.

Because there is a sitting area with a large TV on one side and a pool table on the other, I believe it to be an entertainment/receiving room. Furthermore, this is about the third room of this type.

The Jamesons have it very good.

"That's precisely the reason Jenna has such a large head."

"What?" On my left, Jordan Michaels stops mid-sip from his red cup and gives me a confused look.

My cheeks start to get warm. "I was conversing with myself."

"What?" He grins after repeating. "Are you crazy, or what?"

I remove my shame by rolling my eyes. "Jordan, return home. You're inebriated.

He looks at me, shrugging. "All right."

I give a little shake of my head and turn to look at the boys gathering around the pool table.

No Caleb yet.

I let out an audible breath, relieved.

To be honest, I don't know how I'm going to kiss him. It's not like I can just approach the boy and ask to kiss him.

I mean, I did dress nicely for the occasion. I couldn't possibly show up to Jenna's party looking anything less than flawless. That would be the biggest error in history.

I pulled out the gorgeous little black dress I planned to wear to a formal event. For example, a funeral.

In my opinion, it looks cute on me, at least in the mirror. To go with it, I even styled my long hair into a high ponytail.

But would my efforts even be sufficient to catch Caleb's interest? Sufficient for him to desire a kiss?

To be honest, I don't know him that well. He's incredibly popular because he's the swim team captain and Jenna's ex-boyfriend. He's quite pleasant, I suppose?

The truth is that because Jenna and I have always been at odds, I've never had the opportunity to hang out with him—either at school or outside of it. We stick to our little groups.

I'm not even sure when our hatred for each other began. Just that it started back in elementary school. I believe there was a fancy pencil case involved. Then what, a lunchbox?

The specifics are yet unclear.

Whatever. We now despise one another. That is the only thing involved.

After giving the room another look and failing to see Caleb, I turned and re-entered the corridor. Only to crash into a wall head-on.

"Whoa."

"Hey, observe—" When I find out who the "wall" is, I can no longer say those things. "Caleb!"

His eyes blinked at me. "Hey, Finke, what up?"

I sometimes forget how tall Caleb is. Compared to my five feet six inches, he is one of the tallest guys in the school.

He also has decent looks. He's the cutest boy in the senior class, according to Becca. That may be the case, as I know other gals who feel the same way.

I suppose I also concur with each of them. I'm envious of his long, thick lashes that frame his equally dark eyes, plus he has nice-looking, thick dark hair.

Unquestionably not ugly.

He is Jenna's former lover, though, which means that in the crush department, he's off-limits. Not that I'm scared of her. I simply don't want to interact with her or anyone closely related to her.

When I can speak again, I say, "You're here."

Indeed. Just like you," he quips, then scowls in perplexity. "Anyway, what are you doing here?"

I understand his true request.

I merely shrug. "Your girlfriend invited me."

"Former partner. Don't you detest her soul as well?

I shrug once more.

He finally clears his throat, but not before we stand there for a long while and look at one other awkwardly. "I guess I should go inside now."

"Oh, I see. I give way to allow him to pass and then observe him as he heads towards the pool table. I nibble on my lip. "Well, that didn't work out."

I might be lucky in the future. After all, the night is still young.

****

Lewis and Becca are gone from the pool area when I get back. Most likely, we went inside to socialize with our other students. The Jameson family could live anywhere because of the size of their home.

Finding them is going to be a huge hassle.

Leaving my phone and bag in Lewis's car is not a good idea. Oh no. Why am I such a jumbled forgetter?

I look around to see whether they're still around, but I can't see them.

The couple that made it out is back together and is going strong. I suppose more power to them.

I turn around and go back inside, sighing. However, it doesn't appear that luck is on my side this evening.

Jenna Jameson is staring at me directly from a distance of several feet; she has a shimmering red outfit and a big, cheerful smile. "I'm so happy you came, Nelly."

Hold on. Is she grinning?

To be sure I'm not dreaming, I have to blink a few times.

I never saw Jenna grin at me. At all.

There must be a first for this.

Then, to my utter surprise and terror, she draws nearer and envelops me in her arms.

Alright. What in the world is happening?

When she lets go, my eyes burst out of their sockets.

"I believed you wouldn't survive. However, here you are. I'm very happy you chose to attend. Even though I'm staring at Jenna in disbelief, she smiles.

Why wouldn't I be, too? The girl behaves like we've been friends for a long time, but that couldn't be further from the truth.

"Are you high or what?" I just have to ask.

"What?" Her eyes flicker with irritation so briefly that I almost question whether I'm dreaming this.

"Nearly" is the keyword here.

Jenna is acting fake.

Why is the big, gigantic question?

Is this a corny adolescent film scenario where the evil girl makes friends with the innocent lead character and plans to humiliate her behind her back?

I mean, I'm not a simpleton protagonist. Furthermore, Jenna is too weak to be a decent, cruel girl. Her long blond hair is the sole similarity she has with Regina George. Perhaps the slender figure as well.

However, I wouldn't rule it out for her.

My gaze narrows. "What made you ask me to come here?"

"Silly because I wanted you here."

"Why? Because you intend to take action? I understand it is your birthday, and I wish you a happy birthday. However—

"Jenna, hello!"

I look over my shoulder and see Dana Clancy a few feet away. The redhead is dressed in a glittering garment similar to Jenna's but in gray.

Are these two going to close the evening with a performance?

"Oh, it's Dana." Does Jenna appear relieved to see her pal, or is it just me? "All well, I'll see you around. Have fun at the celebration.

Yes, I reply with a deadpan. After that, observe them leaving together. Isn't that convenient, then? I mumble.

Whatever. Her evil scheme can wait. And she's lame, as I mentioned. She will not be able to pull that off in any manner. Regardless of how complex she perceives it to be.

Like when she decided it would be a good idea to trick me. I won't go into specifics, but it backfired spectacularly on her. I had one of the best days ever.

I'm sure she'll get the same outcome if she ever pulls a similar ruse as I did tonight.

Of course! Here are some further suggestions to carry on with your quest for personal development and betterment:

Develop an optimistic outlook: Learn to be optimistic and to concentrate on the good things in life. This mental adjustment can improve your general wellbeing, wellbeing, and resilience.

Develop mindfulness: Make mindfulness a part of your everyday activities. Take part in mindful eating, deep breathing exercises, or meditation with complete presence and awareness.

Gain proficiency in effective communication: Focus on strengthening your ability to communicate assertively and with active listening. Good communication fosters understanding and strengthens bonds between people.

Increase your knowledge and abilities by consistently looking for chances to learn and develop. To widen your horizons, try taking new classes, reading books on various subjects, or attending conferences and workshops.

Develop wholesome relationships by surrounding yourself with encouraging, upbeat, and inspiring people. Make an effort to spend time and energy developing genuine connections in your relationships.

Practice introspection and self-reflection by making time for these activities. Evaluate your ideas, feelings, and behaviors regularly to learn more about yourself and make the required changes for personal development.

Establish measurable objectives consistent with your values and aspirations to create meaningful goals. Make a plan of action to achieve them and break them down into smaller goals.

Accept lifelong learning: Develop an attitude of ongoing education and development. Accept challenges as chances for growth and be receptive to fresh viewpoints, experiences, and concepts.

Make self-care a priority.

Practice kindness and appreciation: Make it a practice to show others kindness and express gratitude for all the benefits in your life. These activities build a feeling of community and positivity.

Seek assistance when required: Don't be afraid to ask for assistance when faced with difficulties or managing challenging emotions. Asking for assistance from experts, friends, or family is a show of courage and self-awareness.

Accept variety and work toward creating an inclusive environment: Accept diversity in all manifestations. Acquire knowledge from diverse viewpoints and proactively confront assumptions and preconceptions.

Practice time management: Establish deadlines, prioritize tasks, and make a balanced schedule by honing your time management abilities. As a result, stress levels drop, and productivity increases.

Accept failure as a teaching opportunity: Accept failures as important teaching moments and apply them to your strategy to improve it.

Develop self-compassion: Show yourself kindness and compassion, especially when things are hard. Give yourself the same consideration and compassion you would offer a friend who is trying.

Remember that there is no one-size-fits-all strategy for personal growth; it is a lifelong endeavor. Select the tactics that speak to you and modify them to fit your situation. Remain dedicated, practice self-compassion, and acknowledge each accomplishment along your journey toward personal growth.

Of course! Here are some further suggestions to carry on with your quest for personal development and betterment:

Develop an attitude of thankfulness: Give thanks regularly for the things you are grateful for in your life. Maintain a thankfulness diary or set aside time daily to consider your blessings. By engaging in this activity, you can focus more on positivity and improve your general well-being.

Build your resilience by taking on obstacles head-on and persevering through failures. Accept failure as a chance for personal development and make the most of your experiences. Use self-care techniques and get help when needed to get through challenging situations.

Encourage a growth-oriented perspective: Adopt a growth mentality, the conviction that intelligence and skill can be acquired with work and repetition. Accept challenges, keep going in the face of difficulties, and view setbacks as chances to grow and learn.

Exercise regularly: Regular exercise in your regimen will help you feel better physically and mentally. Make time regularly for the things you enjoy doing. You can feel happier, less stressed, and more energy overall when exercising.

Accept creativity: Whether it's writing, painting, playing an instrument, or any other artistic expression, get involved in creative endeavors that let you express yourself. This might give you a sense of fulfillment and enable you to access your inner creative potential.

Show yourself the same attention and consideration as you would a loved one. You can cultivate self-compassion by embracing your flaws, valuing yourself, and taking care of yourself.

Give back by volunteering: Seek opportunities to positively impact your community and contribute. Donate your time, talents, or resources to causes or organizations that share your ideals. Giving back can give one a feeling of fulfillment and purpose.

Maintain a good work-life balance: Give it top priority to balance your professional and personal lives. Establish limits, use your time wisely, and schedule for things you enjoy and find fulfilling outside of work.

Take measured risks: Go outside your comfort zone and take measured chances consistent with your values and aspirations. Take advantage of fresh possibilities, push yourself to do new things, and don't allow fear to stop you from pursuing your goals.

Practice forgiving others and yourself: Let go of grudges and exercise forgiveness. Emotionally draining things are resentment and wrath that you hold onto. By forgiving yourself, you can develop inner peace and rid yourself of bad feelings.

Always be learning and developing: Have an open mind and a lifelong learning attitude. Seek out new information, hone new abilities, and keep up with topics that interest you. This can promote personal development, help you broaden your perspectives, and help you adjust to changes.

Take care of your passions by scheduling time for pursuits and interests that fulfill you and pique your interest. Whether participating in creative endeavors, going on outdoor adventures, or playing sports, pursuing your passions can improve your sense of fulfillment and wellbeing.

Use good stress-reduction techniques: Discover stress-reduction strategies that are good for you, such as mindfulness exercises, relaxation techniques, or leisure activities. Make self-care a priority and try your best to avoid stressful situations.

They get along well and are informed on any relevant news. Naturally, Kate is slower than them.

Shaking her head, she questioned, "What?"

"Had to cover for the homeroom teacher for a while."TuongBeiBei said, "I've heard there's a manpower shortage. Currently, grade eight (*) lacks a homeroom teacher, so we could need to step in for a while."

Eighth grade (初二) (*): China's educational system states that primary school lasts six years, secondary school lasts six years (including middle school and high school), and both lasts six years. Accordingly, the first grade two

(初二) corresponds to Vietnam's eighth grade.

"It's only been over a month since we arrived. The summer break for pupils is almost here. The role of the class president also involves skill development.

Ho Du seemed to be telling Kate what to do as he opened his mouth to speak.

"How was this decided?" Kate inquired.

Yes, she is a little concerned if that is the case.

Being a class president comes with more pressure and duties than just teaching in a classroom. In addition, she had never taught before, much less served as class president.

Honestly, nobody wants to put up with this stall.

"I'm at a loss for how to choose." The opposite was true; grinning, TuongBoi said, "If no one recommends themselves, maybe there will be a draw."

For a brief while, Kate remained mute, continuing to be confused. Ho Du got up, gathered her belongings, and left just as she was about to ask more questions.

"Take advantage of the weekend; I still have to go back and prepare lesson plans to avoid being unable to respond in time."

"I'll accompany you." TuongBeiBei rose swiftly.

When Kate's words came to her lips, she sucked them back.

She genuinely wanted to talk to them about the lesson plan, but it didn't seem like they welcomed her.

After a few periods of silent sitting, Kate packed her bags, got up, and left.

I have to give it to Mrs. Eva, who is here.

She reasoned that she still needed to buy some fruit at the store in front before moving in.

You should act civil when you go out.

Andrew stood outside Third High School for two hours.

Observing the heavens, the night was drawing in.

Adam stood until his legs hurt so much that he could no longer stand, yet he didn't stop moving.

Finally, he was forced to swear, saying, "Andrew, this guy is scum." All he can do is hide if he is unable to fight."

"Let's climb the back wall and go in; give it a good beating first so it remembers it well!"

The youth had on a jacket, his features vague in the shadows. Sitting on the steps with his left leg extended, he stared at the door, breathing solemnly and remaining silent.

It is about six o'clock at night.

The evening self-study period starts at nine o'clock and ends according to summertime.

The Third High School has severe rules. You will not be permitted in if you do not wear the required uniform. They attempted to enter in the afternoon but were thwarted.

You're correct, Andrew. Adam remarked, "Don't you have the school uniform?" after having an epiphany.

"It's been a long time!" Andrew retorted impatiently, pulling down his left leg as he just felt that he was noisy.

"Why would someone drop out of school, keep those ripped clothes, and dress like a fool?" is beyond me.

Everything that was disposed of had previously been disposed of.

Adam hesitated to speak, afraid he would fall into the gun muzzle again. Andrew was not in good humor tonight.

Not sure how much time has passed.

It was pitch black.

Individuals started exiting through the large door. At last, Andrew waited calmly and appeared to lower his head, but his gaze remained fixed on the large entrance.

He was not seeing the folks he was looking for as they walked back and forth.

Andrew had an epiphany after picking up the phone and glancing at the time.

His gaze shifted slightly, and he got up to board the motorbike.

Adam's reaction was met with a "popping" sound. He leaped to his feet and chased after him, his entire body trembling with fear. Screaming, "Andrew, wait for me!" he raced.

Originally, there was only one big door to enter High School #3, but if you looked around and tried a method, you could also unlock a small door close to the gym.

Typically, very few High School No. 3 students are aware of this.

That scumbag Phan Vu is probably going to avoid the large entrance and instead use the smaller one to slip away.

Adam's legs could not match the speed of the motorcycle's two wheels. He was panting fiercely and red-faced as he ran after him. He was unable to even speak, much less yell.

A "Bang" was heard, and the ground appeared to tremble multiple times as he raced to find Andrew tossing a stick there.

Andrew scowled and tugged at the corners of his mouth, giving the impression that he was hurting himself. His eyes were slightly lowered and had a vicious expression.

It appears to have been resolved.

"Andrew, how are you doing?" The sound, according to Adam, also included panting.

"Why even bother running if you can do those things?"

"What a complete scumbag to run away so quickly!"

Andrew simply cursed angrily without responding, got up, and walked away.

Adam was too scared to say anything more.

Andrew has an extremely strong arm, so if he does hit someone, it will hurt. Who can endure it?

It's not a novelty run.

Andrew strolled alongside the motorbike but stayed there for a while, leaning over.

Say nothing at all.

In a desolate lane late at night, two lone figures were reflected in the faint street lights; they seemed unexpectedly calm and frightening.

At last, Adam found himself forced to speak.

Let's return to New York, Andrew. Additionally, you've been kicked out of school. Staying in this district is no longer worthwhile.

Adam gave him some advice.

They want a degree but lack one; they want talent but lack it, and it is not beneficial for them to continue looking for it if they cannot find it.

In the district, it is not appropriate to suggest that something is tiny or large.

They seem to have no intention of doing anything but staying here all day.

Honestly, nobody desires a life like that.

But Andrew remained silent.

Andrew, at least, didn't chastise anyone. After pausing briefly, Adam said, "The university exam is now over. My grandmother must know that I did not take the exam."

Adam spoke very carefully, not wanting to upset Andrew by stating this. He is, after all, currently akin to a firecracker that bursts when ignited.

"What do you mean that I never take the exam and no longer attend school?" "For this little matter, do you have to bother the old lady?" asked Andrew indifferently.

I was in awe when I explored the project house after work. Everything had been reduced to its most basic elements. It was our blank slate to do with as we pleased. As I moved from room to room, ideas for flooring and paint colors raced through my head. Troy's country music was muffled by the few walls separating us, but I could tell he was upstairs.

I looked around the downstairs area and walked upstairs to look for him.

He was nailing down the new subflooring in the master bathroom while on his hands and knees. I studied him momentarily, leaning in the doorway that had been taken apart to the studs like everything else.

Sweat trickled down his temple, and his eyes were fixed intently. His strong arm muscles flexed, and the nail gun's thwack phwakphwak beat interrupted the tune that was playing. When he was done, he leaned back on his haunches, reviewed his work, and used his hand to wipe away the sweat.

I remarked, "It's amazing how much work you accomplished today." "Is there anything you would like me to do tonight?"

As soon as I finished speaking, he turned and smiled at my query. "Two bedrooms still need to be cleaned up."

Out of disdain, I raised the corner of my upper lip. "Excellent. My preferred one.

"Remember that I completed five rooms today without your help."

"I know, but come on, give me a break if I want to." Recall that I put in a lot of effort today as well.

"I'm positive you did—in the comfort of your air-conditioned desk."

I turned to leave, disregarding my strong desire to stay here and chat with Troy, knowing that I would lose this fight. I wrinkled my nose at him. I had to tidy up the bedrooms before I could go home.

However, when I turned to walk away, I felt a tiny tug of resistance high on my left leg, causing me to pause in mid-step. I could relate to the sensation of having my fingernails pulled. "Aim for the shot. No, no, no.

Troy took a worried step forward. "What's off?"

"A nail," I've been discovered.

"Where?"

I gestured to the region where my upper thigh and the bare wood doorway frame met. "This is where."

Troy crouched down in front of me, attempting to assess the circumstances. "I am unable to see it."

"You'll need to follow me from behind."

I tried to flip sideways as best I could, bending towards the nail I was stuck on, but Troy was no little fella. Troy also swiveled to the side but halted when he just put one foot through the threshold.

"Um, Rian?"

"What?"

"It appears that you are occupying more space than normal."

I gave him a fierce look. "What?"

With discomfort, he gestured to his chest. "This is where."

I cast a downward glance. There was hardly any space in the little doorway for Troy to pass me without bumping into my artificially augmented chest and Troy's deep chest. No room.

"Well, feel free to proceed. All of it is padding, anyhow. I'm far more concerned about my beautiful jeans getting destroyed.

"Why not? He held his breath at the beginning of his question and pushed past me. To his credit, he hardly made contact with me at all. "Have you not changed them?"

"After this new guy at work spilled coke on my shirt, I was halfway changed and too lazy to change again." In addition, you removed the doors from every lavatory. Where was I meant to make the change?

"A new employee?"

Indeed. He's this adorable nerd with glasses and all. I believe he may be partially Japanese or Korean. I'm not sure. Yet he has great cheekbones and

Troy crouched down behind me, placing one hand on my hip and nudging me to lean in the opposite direction. Allow me to speculate. You've already asked him out.

"How were you aware of this?"

It wasn't difficult. You and I go back a long way. In addition, this is the first time I have seen you use a bra pad. Don't panic; I'm going to try to unhook you now.

I tried to look over my shoulder and see what he was doing, but I could not. I could only sense how he pressed his fingers against my nail, attempting to pry my jeans loose.

"Slightly bend your knees."

But I paused when I heard the crack of taut strands breaking, even though I was moving slowly. To stabilize myself, I braced my arm against the opposite doorframe and stated, "Just to be clear, I didn't pad my bra—it just came that way." And that meant wearing a sticky one, not wearing one, or both. That was not an option.

All Troy could do in reply was humph. I had to clarify something because he was focused on his assignment.

In any case, what benefit does bra padding provide? After all, someday, someone will find out about the lie if you wind up dating the guy. Where are you then, exactly?

Troy said, "Maybe it makes women feel more confident."

I cast a close look at him. "Thought about this for a while before?"

He shrugged. Not at all. I've never known you to lack confidence, but it's not that difficult to figure out. He placed his hands at my waist and pushed himself back between me and the doorframe. "Cover my neck with your arms right now. I must help you off that nail if we want to salvage your jeans.

Even if his approach made sense, nothing about this circumstance made sense. I felt prickles all over my skin where he touched my waist, and I got a great look at his jawline.

"Rian?"

"Oh." I tried to convince myself that this was Troy as I raised my arms and placed both hands on his neck. The guy who had supported me through all my breakups and early adult mistakes and had been my best friend since high school. He had witnessed me at my worst and was aware of every unpleasant event in my past. He had seen the majority of them. And of him, I could say the same thing. Being this close to him should have been typical, boring, and unperplexing.

"One, two, three." Troy leaned on three, his hands grabbing my waist and slowly raising me.

Troy went to the side and laid me down inside the bedroom again, and I felt one tiny tug on my jeans, but I knew then that I was free. However, for some reason, I held onto him. And he held on to me tightly.

"How is the damage?"

"Injuries?" I stood back, clearing my head with a big breath. Troy's hands gradually withdrew.

Naturally, I couldn't see anything even when I cocked my head about. Feeling told me there was a dime-sized hole somewhat below my panty line. "You've already removed every mirror in the house."

Troy took hold of my shoulders and spun me around to examine it. It is insignificant. When you purchased them, they had larger holes in them.

Shaking his hands off my shoulders, I turned to give him a fierce look. It was he who removed the door's trim and revealed the nail. After all, I bent over to talk to him since he'd given me a strange feeling, mostly because he failed to understand the significance of this. "Not in the behind."

Simply put on a long shirt. Or, you now own an additional pair of work jeans.

"I apologize if I don't want everything in my wardrobe to look like yours." I cast a critical glance at his clothing, which was worn from our past house flips. "And what do you know? You're accurate. I will die alone if I can't figure out how to go past a first date and have a successful relationship. Therefore, I need all the confidence I can get right now.

I forced a smile to my lips, and a tremble to my chin, but Troy only gazed at me. Oh, halt. You will not pass away by yourselves.

"How are you aware of this?"

"Because you will continue to pursue men in the assisted living facility, making it more difficult for them to elude you." Imagine that you won't even be interested in kissing anymore. Who offers you his dessert after supper and his game card on bingo night will be all that matters to you.

I tightened my jaw and took a long breath through my nostrils. "I'm heading to tidy the bedrooms now."

"Avoid stooping over too soon. Those jeans probably can't withstand much more strain.

Overmy-shoulder glares at him weren't nearly pleasing enough. When I needed a door to close, why wasn't there one?

I see nothing but dick when I look at Bryce.

Large penis.

I'm trying not to let it show at this wedding, but I can't help but think of the sensation of his meat pressing firmly against my thigh in his hotel room.

I catch Bryce's gaze staring at me for a moment. I felt his gaze pull me in, thick like a collar around my neck. The image of him in his hotel room, his nude form imprinted like a brand, keeps coming back to me.

I wonder what it would be like to give in and let myself be consumed by his flames after having sexual thoughts inspired by the image. His breath burned hot and heavy across my skin, like a summer storm about to blow. My heart thuds in my chest, resonating throughout the space like a drumbeat. I try to eliminate the idea, but it's like a stain that won't go away no matter how often I scrub.

I get excited and scared simultaneously when I consider giving in. I haven't been looked at like Bryce looks at me in a very long time, as though he'd like to eat me whole.

Get out there and get a fling, my mother advised, but damn. I had no idea it would happen so quickly. Not at work, either.

I take refuge in the bride's dressing room to avoid his lewd looks. Semaj, James' sister, enters the dressing room with her hair still moist from a recent shower, giving the impression that she has been up since the previous night—at least, I hope so. I'll take that over the other two ladies who are nowhere to be found. I led Semaj to the hair and cosmetics department and started looking for Shade and Tiffany.

With my phone out, I send them a polite reminder via text that they are already ten minutes late for cosmetics and hair appointments. When the doors suddenly open and the two women enter carrying four glasses and a pitcher of sangria, my thumb hovers over the send button.

I put my phone down and grabbed Shade's spectacles. As soon as I set them on the table, Tiffany began to fill them. Her bridal dress hangs inches from the table, so I swiftly adjust it.

Tiffany extends her glass towards me. "I appreciate you putting everything together. James and I are astounded by how much you accomplished in such a short time.

I accept the glass gracefully, but I won't drink anything just now. Since I'm still technically working, I want to ensure nothing goes wrong.

James requested that I just be a guest and take the day off. He ought to have realized it wasn't going to occur. I couldn't leave the specifics to anyone else because it's a big day for him.

I smile and respond, "It was nothing." "I just want to ensure that today is something you two will remember fondly."

Tiffany gives me a warm congratulations on my work. James and I may not have had the finest past, but we are still like family. I won't allow my prior disagreements with Tiffany to stop me from making today truly memorable.

At first, I had doubts about Tiffany's intentions with James. But she exudes love for him as I observe her surrounded by pals who all smell like sangria.

With a dreamy smile playing at the edges of her lips, she continues, "He's just the most amazing man I've ever met." "I have no idea how fortunate I became to have him in my life."

She truly loves James, contrary to my previous belief that she only used him for his security and wealth. She refers to James as though he were her shining hero.

Taking another glass of sangria, Tiffany says, "I just want to make him happy and do everything I can to support him." "Even though I know I don't deserve him, I refuse to let him go."

In sharp contrast to the Tiffany, I believed I knew this one. Her eyes convey the truth, and that makes me feel good. The burden of my doubts has been lifted, and a switch has been flicked. We raise our glasses together and toast the future, Mrs Davis.

I break out of the dressing room before they can tempt me with more drinks and jokes. I make my way to the groom's changing area.

The men wear their suits to the maximum, so I pause to catch my breath.

My wedding memories come rushing back. Not quite as intricate as this was mine. Under a Kohl's dress, there was just the small baby belly and Greg and me. The first time I washed my hands after marriage, my finger turned green from our inexpensive rings. I never gave a damn about it.

Nevertheless, I adored it. In addition to many other things, Greg offered to purchase me a better one. We simply never made it there.

I shake my head violently to shrug off the memory and walk over to the men.

I see Bryce chit-chatting with Tiffany's relatives as I approach the group, acting like he's known them for years. I'm intrigued by the effortless confidence with which he speaks to the wedding party while not being a member of it. Even though I know he is an old friend of hers, I wonder how close her family was to him.

I can't help but be curious. I'll excuse James and myself to have a quiet conversation with him.

"Are you prepared for this now?" I ask, chuckling.

"As prepared as I'll ever be," James chuckles nervously. "I appreciate you taking on everything. I truly appreciate everything you've done to make our family feel at ease. You've gone above and above.

I ignored his praise and redirected the discussion to why I pulled him aside. "What's wrong with Bryce?" I nod towards Bryce as I pose my question. He's conversing with them as though he were a family member.

Speaking a little disoriented, James says, "I told you they go way back."

"Really?" I inquire, astonished. "I had no idea they had such a long history."

James laughs. He shrugs and says, "Yeah, they used to date in high school or something."

My mouth falls open. I am not familiar with this. All I can say is, "Oh," when asked.

I think James senses my astonishment when he asks, "Are you into him?" James shoots me a sidelong glance and gets serious. Hello, how are things going for you right now?

I am fully aware of what he is discussing. "James, I'm OK. Putting on a brave face, I answer, "Don't worry about me.

Before he could say anything further, I put my hands on his arms and offered him a comforting squeeze. He seems skeptical. "I swear, I'm alright. Admire your in-laws, please. Please don't stray too far, as we're about to start.

James nods and joins the group again, laughing and chatting with Bryce, not seeming to be affected by his and Tiffany's previous connection.

Bryce's gaze is back on me for some reason. His eyes follow every curve of my body, making time slow down. His tongue twitches out to moisten his mouth. Like a lion pursuing its prey, his unflinching gaze locked upon me. My heart is pounding so hard in my chest that I feel compelled to jump.

At that moment, a group member claims his attention. That tells me it's time to return to work.

***

I hear the soft notes of a live R&B song played on an acoustic guitar as I push open the great doors to the ballroom. The sounds swirl and dance throughout the space, ambiance-setting the wedding with a dreamlike feel.

The guests enter and are astounded by the enchanted scene before them. The fairy lights interwoven into the floral garlands above create an ambiance of warmth and intimacy, making it ideal for commemorating the marriage of two souls.

Each chair is arranged in a half circle around the platform of the bride and groom so that everyone can see them. The gentle flicker of candlelight on each table highlights the faces of the attendees. A divine fragrance wafts through the air like tender sentiments of love, placed in exquisite vases with blush pink peonies and creamy white roses.

A regal atmosphere is created by the bride and groom's décor, which includes gold highlights, flowing white drapes, and a delicate chandelier glittering above the dance floor. I made a great effort to ensure everything was planned to create the ideal celebration of love. As

I take it all in, my heart is bursting with happiness and excitement for the pair.

As I distributed the wedding itinerary at the door, Bryce sneaked by me. I extend my hand to take his arm. His fitted suit feels so far different from my casual clothes. As the light reflects off the diamonds on his watch, I become acutely aware of our world's differences.

There were a lot of accomplished individuals who I shook hands with while working at that front desk. An Italian suit and a high-end watch are easily recognizable to me. I mentally calculate how long I would have to pay for any of that, making me feel vulnerable and intimidated.

But then I feel excitement come over me as he grabs the wedding schedule from my hand. He puts his soft, warm fingers around mine, gradually drawing me closer. As he gets closer, the subtle smell of his cologne transports me back to his hotel room, complete with a frontal of Bryce. I could sprint a marathon on him; that's how energizing and invigorating the fresh citrus aroma is.

He stoops to murmur in my ear, radiating heat from his body. "Seek me out later, my love."

I try not to get too worked up, but I can feel the tension rising between my legs and my heart racing.

I'm not strong.

He has finally addressed any unspoken issues that may have existed between us. I try to ignore my emotions and concentrate on the wedding, but as soon as I see the piercing look in his eyes, I realize I won't be able to last the night without breaking.

The Greek term CIEL means "heaven," precisely what this opulent residential skyscraper with 100 stories will be. My goal in doing this project is to elevate the standard of American real estate and establish Grayson Inc. as a formidable entity. I'm grateful.

The room bursts into cheers as the lights come back on, as they ought to.

As I head for my seat, I hear comments like "Bravo!" and others. It's next to

Grayson Inc.'s Executive Chairman and CEO, or, as I would like not to say, "my dad."

The board meeting is finally adjourned, and the directors depart in unison, leaving the four higher-ups alone for a post-meeting conversation. To my surprise, Carl Wiggins, a crucial board member, receives longer applause, which almost instantly turns sour when he talks. "What a presentation that was! Mr. Grayson, your son, is a remarkable young man. You had to feel incredibly proud.

Richard Grayson concurs, "I guess he's a chip off the old block," to which the other men chuckle hysterically.

My mood is officially off right now. It's been months since I put forth this much effort to stand in Richard Grayson's shadow again. In addition to being the CEO of Grayson Inc.'s only son, Devon Grey, I'm also the dazzlingly bright future of American real estate. Ciel is my creation—my idea. Not 'the son of my father.' I detest that tag so much. It's not useful to me.

I have earned every million dollars I possess, I manage a tight ship of businesses across the shores of New England, and I'm a year away from graduating from Thackeray's School of Business at the top of my class. Nothing at all was taken from Richard Grayson's back. Few guys my age have accomplished enough to be seated at this table. I should be treated as a man of my caliber, but what the fuck do I get?

Another board member, Harris, says, "He's a wizard, gents." "Our pride is in you, son. Continue your fantastic work.

Son? Fire me.

Richard Grayson does as one would anticipate and takes pleasure in this farce. He thinks it's important to constantly remind me of my "place" if I start harboring odd ideas.

Similar to, say, a hostile takeover of my father's company.

Incredibly feasible and seductive as fuck, but this isn't the right time. I've been giving the old man the runaround for years, and I won't change until I'm ready to make my big Grayson Inc. debut.

Harris inquires, "I understand you're heading to Rocky Cove tomorrow."

"Today," I reply. I should invite you to one or the other game, but what else are beaming, proud dads good for?

Richard Grayson steps up to the plate with ease. "Watch Devon play football; it's amazing." Devon is excellent at more than just real estate.

If nothing else, he acknowledges my outstanding sportsmanship. Also merited.

Despite appearances, it is a facile assumption that I despise my father. I'm not. You are right, Though we don't have the perfect father-son relationship. We never carried it out.

It's simple to put that down to the fact that my thinking was completely open when I was much younger, and Richard Grayson was never present. Luckily, I saw early on that his obsession was not being a dad but becoming the best at his business. So, instead of becoming mad at him, I accepted the cue and made a name for myself in the same field.

My father and I are a deadly combination when our interests collide, even though our filial relationship isn't quite on track. For example, we purchased one of our longstanding competitors last year following the death of its CEO. The company desperately needed acquisition after falling into horribly inadequate hands. Such an opportunity presented itself, and we could not let it slip into the hands of other corporate predators. Although we paid what losers call "dirt cheap," it was a significant investment. It is now a devoted division of Grayson Inc. A profit-puffing monster, in which I own fifty percent along with Richard Grayson.

My father and I would have an emotional link if my mother, who also happens to be his wife, could deliver her lungs on a platter rimmed with gold. Who needs that when we can connect over money, corporate purchases, and mergers?

To be fair, Richard and I have gone to several formal functions and business conferences together. A few years ago, we also looked adorable on the Forbes cover. That kind of thing has to make up for bear hunting, fishing, or whatever other father-son pastimes are these days.

Well, the holidays are gone, so say goodbye to this pit of misery and the constant need to stare each other down. The Rocky Cove coastlines provide a lot of exciting things to look forward to. I was born to answer the call of the good life, which includes my independence, exclusive social circle, penthouse, business, bundles of cash ready to be made, and a new football season.

Chapter 4: Luke's Arrival

Luke Reynolds arrived at Seabreeze Inlet, a hamlet where time seemed to stop and reflect on the gentle lap of waves. That day, everything about the village was forever altered. On this late spring eve, the sun had just set, casting long shadows across the cobblestone streets and painting the sky in hues of pink and lavender.

Luke was unlike any other person the town had ever seen. He arrived like a cool sea breeze, providing much-needed refreshment and a dash of intrigue. He was tall and slim, his chestnut hair reflecting the tone of the sand beside the water, and he moved with a calm assurance that seemed at odds with Seabreeze Bay's tranquility.

He had chosen a quirky house near the beacon for his temporary haven, and he anticipated finding solace there from a past he had hidden away. Luke enjoyed that few understood the underlying reasons for his look. His background was fiercely guarded and concealed behind those piercing blue eyes that revealed unspoken secrets.

The locals could not resist the chance to gossip about the bewildering newbie. While some merely found him beautiful, others made assumptions about his experiences. It seemed that Luke had an insinuating smile, a captivating aura that defied explanation.

To his terrible surprise, his trip to Seabreeze Bay, a village that seemed stuck in the past, would coincide with the presence of a certain woman named Emma. Their paths would eventually meet, and in that lucky meeting, their lives would never be the same as desires and secrets intertwined in ways neither of them could have predicted.

Chapter 5: The Unexpected Relationship

That evening, the sea air had cooled off and carried a hint of salt as it rustled through the palm tree leaves that blanketed the shore. Emma hadn't anticipated anything unusual that evening as she strolled along the shore, enthralled by her views. However, fate had other ideas.

Emma's path inadvertently brought her closer to Luke's cabin near the beacon as the waves gently touched the coast. Her attention was caught by the subtle shimmer coming from his window and cascading down the cobblestone path. She could not resist a curious glance.

Through that window, she saw a life devoid of routine and full of scrutiny and isolation—a life she had never experienced before. Luke sat at a worn-out wooden table beneath the warm glow of a single light, keeping a sketchbook close at hand. His expression seemed very focused as he refreshed his area of expertise.

Time seemed to stop as their eyes met through the glass. Emma couldn't explain the electric charge that flowed between them at the moment, but it was undeniable. Perhaps the cosmos had planned to bring two spirits together in the most unexpected way.

She continued to look, and Luke sensed her presence and slowly turned to face upward. Their gaze met, and everything around them became insignificant. A silent understanding drifted between them, unspoken words swirling in the sea wind.

Emma's heart raced as she jerked her gaze away and continued walking down the beach. Although the encounter was short-lived, it left a lasting impression on her. She genuinely desired to contemplate the stranger holding the sketchbook, considering their connection during that silent moment.

She was shocked to learn that this chance encounter would be the spark that ignited a fire inside of her, a fire that would test her emotions and take her in a direction she had never anticipated—one of self-disclosure and love.

Teenage Awakening

The second chapter of "The Journey of the First Kiss" takes us on the intriguing adventure of adolescence, a period of great discovery, progress, and perplexity for our heroes, Jane and David. This chapter is a patchwork of the many feelings, encounters, and changes of growing up.

We watch as Jane and David negotiate the challenges of middle school, including peer pressure, the need to fit in, conflicting emotions, and sporadic bouts of loneliness. Their relationship, hitherto characterized by its innocence, becomes increasingly complex. They begin to see their affection for one another differently, which thrills and terrifies them.

Jane, the spirit of perpetual adventure, throws herself into the maelstrom of puberty. She's maturing emotionally and physically. She still has the same daring energy but has a new depth and maturity that she lacked as a child. She starts to recognize David more as a boy and as a friend. She observes how his voice cracks when he's worried; his eyes light up when he talks about his favorite books, and how warmth fills the room when he's around.

In contrast, David stays silent and contemplative, yet beneath his composed façade lies a turbulent underbelly. He's unsure how to deal with his more intense feelings for Jane. He keeps a distance from her, stealing glances and savoring their brief exchanges. His tongue knots up, his palms sweat, and his pulse flutters whenever she's around—all telltale indicators of a young boy in love.

This chapter's most remarkable incident takes place at the yearly school dance. Jane looks stunning when she wears a lovely blue dress that complements her eyes. David is afraid and in awe of her once he gets a fresh perspective. Despite his heart's desire, his dread of being rejected prevents him from asking her out.

But as the evening wears on, David gets up to ask Jane to dance. They dance together in a lovely, awkward way, their hearts pumping in time with the melody. This dance turns into a turning point in their journey that marks the beginning of their youthful love and goes beyond their childhood bond.

David glances into Jane's eyes as they sway to the music, and everything else disappears for a second. Only the two are nestled in their little universe under the dark lights. Even after the dance, the moment remains, offering a glimpse of what's to come.

The relationships between Jane and David change in the days following the dance. They discover that they exchange more grins, sneaking looks, and even flushing when they are around one another. Their feelings had been dormant until the dance, the spark that forced them to surface.

Through her diary entries, where she acknowledges that she is nervous around David, the readers are given a glimpse into Jane's emotional state. She considers how her feelings for her childhood buddy have changed and confides in her concern that these new feelings would cause them to lose their connection.

David expresses his affection for Jane less outwardly yet makes it clear by his behavior. He starts to show more concern for Jane and interest in her interests, and, most crucially, he starts to find the guts to tell Jane how he feels.

Afterward, the chapter opens with a touching moment in which David gives Jane a locket for her birthday. Though modest in size, the present is meaningful and well-intentioned.

An enduring witness to their friendship is their photograph in the locket, taken beneath the old oak tree. David's kindness moves Jane, and keeps the locket as a keepsake of their relationship.

When Matt, a new student, shows in, the chapter unexpectedly takes a different turn when things are going well. Matt is friendly, gregarious, and instantly well-liked, grabbing Jane's interest and making David jealous. David is faced with the prospect of losing Jane for the first time. This evokes a strong range of feelings, including insecurity, jealousy, and dread.

"Why am I seeing a video of you on my FYP that went viral?" The next morning, Riley makes demands during breakfast, and I freeze.

Fantastic. My baby sister has seen the stupid video. She keeps complaining about it now. She's the true drama queen between us, and I know I'm dramatic. Moreover, she is just twelve years old.

As I eat my cereal, I glare at her. "Scroll down and disregard it. It's not like it's difficult.

"I am unable to." My buddies will see this. She complains, sounding as though she has been wronged, "It's so embarrassing."

She didn't even show up.

Ah, yes, drama queen.

Our mother frequently refers to us as her "mini-me." Even though I detest to say it, she's not entirely incorrect. Riley is my younger twin, although by a few years. She has my eyes and hair, although hers are a paler gray.

Since neither of us resembles our parents, I would assume that we were adopted if it weren't for the fact that we are exact replicas of our deceased paternal grandmother. However, Riley used to believe that way. And I would frequently "encourage" that belief, just like any other elder sister. And she was always duped by it.

Regretfully, she has moved past that stage.

"You little brat, how do you think I feel?"

"You didn't need to cover him in that juice."

"Refrain from starting." I glare at them.

Dad enters the kitchen just as she rolls her lovely gray eyes at me.

"What are you two arguing about so early in the morning?" He's already dressed in his work clothes, his thick black hair perfectly combed, while Riley and I are still in pajamas.

My sister may not know, but I don't want to risk staining my school clothing.

I tell our Dad, shoving a spoonful of Froot Loops into my lips, "Riley's just being a brat."

Riley narrows her eyes at me, and before she even opens her mouth, I know what she will say. "Finley's gone viral on TikTok."

Well, I'm going to murder her.

For what purpose? Dad calls this type of speech "Gen Z speak," and he already knows it well.

"Someone recorded her making out with a guy in the school cafeteria."

"What?" Just as I yell, "I did not!" Dad starts barking.

Dad adjusts his glasses with black frames. "Finley, explain."

Yes, that's right. Michael Hart is enraged and perhaps even taken aback. He doesn't get shocking news about his sixteen-year-old daughter very often.

Not that it's scandalous, mind you. Simply embarrassing.Extremely, extremely embarrassing. I still haven't bothered to see it since I don't want to relive it, but my sister's loud mouth has forced me to view it.

I try to play it down, though. It was insignificant, Dad. It was merely an incident. Furthermore, there was no true kiss. Just a brief kiss.

Riley adds, "And then she attacked the guy."

"Quit chatting!" I yell at her. Why do you act like such a brat?

"Because you are awful."

"Well, you're even worse."

"You—" "Enough." We are both biting our tongues in response to Dad's harsh tone. Riley and I instantly comply with him when he uses it, even though he doesn't always. "We're out of time to talk about that trending video. It's time for you both to prepare for school. Finally, though, we'll discuss this more later.

Riley sneers mockingly, "Someone's in trouble," just for my ears while Dad gets up to make himself some coffee.

She would be lying on the kitchen floor right now if appearances could kill.

Ugh. Now, what should I do?

****

"You think your dad will talk you out of it when you come home?" Myles queries her as she bites into her pizza.

"Why do you suppose I remain here?" I say, "No offense, Reen," to Serena. I adore your house.

Serena chuckles. It's alright. You can even spend the night, as I mentioned. My folks won't object.

Yes, I am aware. Her parents, especially her mother, love me. That is both Myles and me. This house used to host many of our sleepovers, and we're currently hanging out in Serena's room. She has a half-eaten pizza box on her bed, and Mean Girls is on her TV, just like our previous sleepovers.

Oh, how I miss those evenings.

Anyway, Serena proposed that we come right here after school after I informed the girls about my sister snooping on me and my Dad wanting to talk to me about it.

I informed my mother over the phone that I would work on a project. Before Dad could even take the phone from Mom and insist that I get home, I abruptly interrupted the call since I could hear him in the background.

Not that he couldn't contact me directly via phone or text. But he still hasn't blown up my phone after about an hour. I'm hoping that he has already moved on from the dumb video.

Riley is foolish and has a foolish mouth.

However, I'm not going home just yet to be safe.

"I long for our sleepovers." I sulk, reaching for another piece and taking a big bite off of it.

"You know what, right?" Myles concurs. "Anyway, when was the last time we had one? Not even I can recall.

Serena calls it her "freshman year." "I recall it because Jared Blinsky had dumped me earlier that day." You two spent the night here because you wanted to lift my spirits.

I blink several times before the memories come back. Yes, that is correct. I can now recall. A frown creases my brow. "Stupid Jared. To think he'd just given you your first kiss a week before he dumped you. What a jerk."

Myles nods. "Boys are jerks. Which is why I'm staying single until college."

Serena and I share a look.

"What?"

I turn to Myles after telling Serena, "I'll take this one." "Don't you have this flirtatious relationship with Thomas Crank going on?"

"Not at all now." She frowns. "A few days ago, I caught him making out with Brianna Murdoch in front of her locker."

"Are you certain?" Serena queries. "Perhaps they were merely conversing."

Her hair was tucked behind her ear by him.

"Very flirtatious," I cringe. I apologize, Myles. Considering exacting revenge? I'll gladly set Dean aside for a moment and focus my wrath on him.

"Right now, he's probably at Dean's house."

Serena and I turn to face her.

And why do you think that, exactly? I insist.

"Because Dean is currently hosting a party there."

"And how do you know this?"

"A week ago, out of neighborly courtesy, he asked if I wanted to come because he lives a few houses down."

He let out another laugh. "Your tongue is attached to a cat?"

Still, I was unable to express myself or act.

"No, your tongue is not shared by a cat. He said, "I do," whirling me around as he swiftly sucked my tongue and ate my mouth.

Nick was very skilled at kissing, and he was free to use my tongue whenever he pleased. I was also his to have whenever he pleased. Marlow was dead on. Whenever I saw him, I hoped he would be my first love and wondered if it would ever pass.

I will settle for his kisses for now, though. He smiled contentedly into my eyes as soon as he withdrew, and I could breathe. He muttered, "Happy belated birthday," and then released his hold on me.

"Whoa, what a surprise for my birthday," I said. "May I also have my birthday tomorrow?" I laughed aloud.

He raised an eyebrow. "Perhaps," he replied before picking up my dropped containers. "It would have mattered, I told you."

I was confused when I stared at him.

He chuckled. Did you find that kiss confusing? I informed you that your birthday would have been significant.

"Oh, that," I laughed and said.

"Rory, keep me updated on anything significant. He put the containers on the counter and returned to work, saying, "I want to know."

The man was quite good at kissing and made me forget my name, but he was also really perplexing. It was enjoyable to flirt with each other. I knew it wasn't serious, no matter how much I wanted it to be. I was going home alone at the end of the day, so why would he want to know about vital things? I could wishful think all I wanted.

I didn't want to think about those things since I'd had enough sleepless nights over them. I would only take away the positive aspects and emotions and be content with them right now.

There was more fear for tomorrow. or perhaps the following. I might as well survive the upcoming week or month since, despite my best efforts to keep it safe, my heart was in it.

Twelve days became weeks, and those weeks became months. With Nick, things were always the same. He'd been so sparing with the kisses that I constantly wondered when the next one would arrive. A few here, a few there—it was never certain. The touchy-feely stuff continued, but my need for more increased as time passed. I gradually began to approach him more, though not to the point where I could just snatch a kiss right out from under him.

I had almost given up on the idea that I would be able to call him mine, but Marlow and Rachel persuaded me to go on a date with a schoolboy who had been persistently making advances.

It was a decent date with Craig. Just like we were buddies, I enjoyed it. I knew right away that there wouldn't be any romantic feelings, and there were none at all because somebody else kidnapped my heart.

Rachel and Marlow tried politely reminding me that I needed to push myself into something new because this thing with Nick had lasted too long. I completely comprehended their perspective. I would have given them the same advice if it had been one of them, but there is always a double standard when it comes to you.

But I forced myself to go out with Craig again, for our sakes. We had gone to the movies and then out for ice cream on our first date. Two weeks later, we went on our second date; this time, he took me to miniature golf. I enjoyed the relaxed chat, which helped me forget about Nick, at least for now. We played mini golf, then he got us smoothies, and we had a stroll around the park. My hand was taken in his. I wished it was Nick, but I forced a grimace on him. It would not be easy.

I made Marlow and Rachel swear not to tell Nick about our two dates with Craig, and I hadn't informed him about them either. Even though I knew it would be foolish to hope for Nick, it was difficult to let go entirely.

Two weeks had passed since Craig and I went on our second date. We hadn't gone out together since, between his and my jobs, and some diversion on my part. Our plans were set for Saturday night. We had scheduled a double date with Erick and Marlow. Marlow's suggestion, hence changing the date, was not an option.

It was a bittersweet Saturday morning. As usual, I was excited to work with Nick, but I wasn't excited about the night I was going on a date with Craig. After working with Nick all morning, it was going to be difficult to concentrate on

Craig. I had about canceling, but I knew Marlow would kill me.

I was working with Sam and Nick once again today. A new part-time manager was being trained by Sam. an arrogant man named David. Within an hour of entering the office, he pretended to know everything because he had worked with Jalisa the previous evening.

I hadn't received a kiss from Nick in a very long time. I was going to pick it up from him today or Craig tonight because I was past due, which was untrue. There was never anything I asked of Craig. I tried to like him differently, but it didn't work.

I made every effort to get a kiss all morning. I would go by very closely. My breasts would slip along him, that close. When he said something humorous, I would playfully swat him, and I would touch him when he spoke to me. Nothing was successful!

David mentioned that Nick and I were experiencing sexual tension during our morning break. Nick laughed, but I felt like puking. I was annoyed that Nick ignored it without looking at me, even though it was 100% accurate.

We completed our last-minute preparations after our break, and Sam and David then opened the doors. While Saturdays weren't as crowded as Sundays in the morning, some customers did come in. An hour would pass before the main surge arrived.

A huge surprise entered the building through the door after Nick had gone to the back to check on some things. Craig. I swiftly made my way to him as I started to fear.

I started to speak, but Craig saw me first. "Hello," he grinned broadly. "I intended to surprise you,"

"Wow," I uttered tremblingly. "You caught me off guard." I looked around, hoping to see Nick, but happily, he wasn't there.

His gaze trailed me. I apologize, but I can't hold you here to avoid trouble. I only wanted to say hello," he remarked with such tender compassion.

Why couldn't I fall in love with such a nice guy like him? I hoped he would get the hint and get out of there by saying, "No worries, the big rush will be here soon."

He grinned. Then he held my hands and leaned in to say, "I'll see you later."

He was going to kiss me, oh my god. I was completely unprepared for that. I was overcome with panic. I was overcome with regret. I never ought to have accepted a second date. I knew that I wouldn't be prepared until this issue between Nick and me was settled.

I was unable to kiss Craig. I was no longer able to play along with him. I tried to turn at the last second so he could kiss my cheek, but I was too slow.

My mouth, his lips touched every corner. Suddenly, I withdrew and planted a kiss on his cheek.

I noticed the look of surprise in his eyes as he withdrew. Nick was standing there, too. Observing us. I let out a sigh and looked down. Craig turned to check why I was acting strangely once he spotted me.

"Oh," he sobbed as he let go of my hands. "I understand. I guess we won't be hanging out together this evening.

"Craig," I murmured. "I apologize. Although he and I are not together, However, what? I was at a loss for words. Besides, there was nothing I could say to improve it.

He turned back and walked out, saying, "Bye, Aurora."

I knew I had made a huge mistake, yet I still stayed there, staring at the door as he left. It wasn't that I would regret dating him; more like I would regret dating him in the first place. Not because I played him but because he wasn't a good guy; in fact, he was. Similar to what Nick was doing to me. I was completely insane.

Nick said nothing as he passed. I was unable to look at him. I felt bad for Craig, and considering what had happened with Justin, I knew Nick would be upset and that we would fight. I decided to find something else to do, like wallowing in my sadness, so I went to the rear instead of returning to my station at the breakfast bar.

It took me a whole minute in the kitchen before Nick wandered back. Shutting my eyes, I inhaled deeply, bracing myself for a fight. His distance from my face measured millimeters when I opened my eyes.

He replied, "I want you to see this coming," and then he grabbed my mouth and ripped it apart. His lips were soft and understanding. He swept my tongue away with his tongue, slipping it inside my mouth, then wrapped his lips around it and sucked.

He withdrew, and I looked into his mouthwatering eyes. "Why? I expected you to be furious.

A carefree smile lit up his face. "It's difficult to be angry when I know you wish I had kissed you instead of him."

My heart gave out. He should know the hurt that runs through me, so I wasn't sure whether to be joyful or angry since he understood exactly how I felt. He plays me while he gets the best of both worlds, even though he knows I desire him.

I told him, "I wish you would just tell me to stop liking you."

"It would be nice if I could also," he sighed. "Rory, I can't, though."

He pulled me in and gave me a deep hug. For the first time since I began to feel lust for him, I sincerely wished he would just let me go. I wasn't in love with him even though I hadn't been able to cling to him for all this time. Nope, things were becoming worse.

Just in time for the crush, we returned to the buffet. Fortunately, the whole shift was packed. I had no time to consider Nick or Craig. Well, other than collaborating with Nick. Only Nick and I left after our shift ended because Sam kept training David. I was expecting an invitation to get a bite to eat in our booth, but I never received one.

I found it difficult to look Nick in the eyes as he led me outside to my truck. That is, until he put a hand under my chin and motioned for me to face him. Something about his gaze seemed odd. It was hardly the typical look of passion. I was unable to locate the additional item.

In a whisper, he said, "Rory, do you want me to tell you to stop liking me?"

I wasn't prepared for that. I was out with this. Knowing that he wouldn't pursue me further, I could leave. He had finally concluded that I couldn't date anyone as long as he was in charge. I had to tell him to get out of my way.

However, I was unable to.

I whispered, "No," barely audible. The words wouldn't come out the way I wanted them to. Not able to.

He also remained silent. Rather, he pressed my lips to his and gave me a kiss he had never given before. Beyond that, it was difficult to articulate.

Five: The Smack

Timing: Recognize that knowing when the moment is right is difficult. You've caressed her, congratulated her, and maybe even laughed a little. Now you're wondering if she's ready for a kiss.

You can check for the following items, which may provide you with hints:

Do you get the impression that she feels at ease with you?

Has she been conversing with you and attentively listening?

Does she find your jokes funny?

Has she been making contact with you?

Is she looking at you with her eyes?

Is she playing tricks on you?

Does she approach you closely?

When she looks at you, do her eyes seem heavy and soft?

Does she have her lips biting or licking?

The ideal location

Though it's not a terrible idea to choose somewhere peaceful and romantic, virtually any setting can work if you have a connection. If she has family at home, please don't wait until you reach her doorstep. Take a stroll in the park and make a halt beside a lake or under a tree. Are you a citizen of the nation? What about a hike in a forest or a view of mountains? Think about visiting a museum or gallery on a calm day in the city. Beside a waterfall or a fountain. In a cable car, on a bridge, on a balcony at dusk.

One of my favorite first kisses was on a bustling Saturday night on Las Olas Boulevard in Fort Lauderdale, Florida. People had no choice but to go around us, even crossing the street. Although the relationship didn't work out, it was a cordial breakup, and I always remember that kiss.

Moving in: Moving confidently and easily may be the most crucial aspect. Additionally, don't forget to breathe!

Most women find it quite appealing when you cup their chin with one hand. It also poses no hazard at all when you lower your other hand. Next, give these methods a try:

Take two or three seconds to look into her eyes, then move your attention to her lips before looking back into them. Now that you have made your intentions clear to her approach cautiously while maintaining eye contact.

As you approach, turn your head to the side slightly, whichever way seems most comfortable. Instead of speaking directly to each other, you don't want to bump noses.

Your lips should only slightly part. Now that your mouth is soft and your jaw is relaxed, you should close your eyes.

Keep your lips gently touching (I know, but it's vital). Plant two or three quick kisses, and then linger on the kiss for a short while. Slowly step back, open your eyes, and give her another glance. You can probably follow her lead at this point. Just let her go if she looks away or moves her head elsewhere. If she maintains eye contact, place your free hand on her back to bring her closer to you before sharing another kiss. You might speak up more this time, but pay close attention to the woman's reaction and avoid overdoing it.

Placing your hands softly on either side of her neck is another gentle method to approach her initially, rather than cupping her chin. Additionally, you could gently pat her cheeks with your thumbs.

And now for a small trick that will add a bit more magic. Pull away from the woman and raise your hand such that your forefinger touches her lips. It ought to be a transient action, so slight that she hardly notices it.

Become an expert at making out.

To be honest, a lot of people in today's hook-up culture have sex before they've even learned the skill of kissing or making out. It's highly possible that you won't go back to fill in the blanks if you rush into sex instead of enjoying the excitement of getting to know each other better. It is doubtful that your partner will attempt it later if it wasn't that essential to them before you had sex. You are very obviously setting expectations for the future when you say that your sex life is essential to you and that you are the kind of person who appreciates the "Million Things." You may discover that your spouse is a 6-minute man or that she is not interested in making you feel good about yourself verbally if they do not want to spend the time to get to know you personally. Several things might be discovered early in the dating process that could later be deal breakers. According to a fascinating study published in the Journal of Sex Research, couples engaged in 11–13 minutes of foreplay and 7-8 minutes of intercourse on average. The couples' desire for twice as much sex time won't come as a surprise to most individuals.

A prospective partner will always be intrigued and ask, "What the heck are the Million Things?" when you tell them you are exploring the Million Things before moving on to sex. Better sex is fueled by desire, which is fueled by curiosity. Indeed, we have all heard of individuals who confessed to having sex on their first date and then claimed to be content after three or even thirty years of marriage. Of course, one must wonder, given that the divorce rate for first marriages ranges from 40 to 50%, and for second marriages, from 60% to 73%.

The best thing about this voyage is that you will know you are sexually and, in many other ways, compatible when you reach your destination. You spend so much time communicating, exploring each other's bodies and preferences, and sharing kisses that you have amassed a vast inventory of potential future developments. On a first or third date, there is never the same amount of trust, intimacy, or connection you have fostered.

People enjoy facts. Thus, one of the most frequently asked questions is, "How long does it take to do a million things?" Reaching the one million milestone is theoretical because, hopefully, your entire body, mind, and spirit are involved in the action. This means that you are doing multiple things at once. The truth is that you can spend as much time as you both wish. In a TimeOut poll conducted in 24 locations, 11,000 respondents were asked, "After how many dates is it appropriate to have sex?" The average number of dates that people should wait to kiss is two dates and 3.53 dates before having sex, according to TimeOut respondents. This implies that, on average, you only go on one more date following your first kiss before having sex! Most people are still only learning the barest details about one another and have no idea what would turn their spouse on.

The need for sex can frequently result in unfulfilling relationships and a sense of estrangement. Everybody has the right to experience the joy of having their needs met completely, from top to bottom.

The most sensual and ideal form of sex is the full-body, mind, and soul encounter. Quickies and sex, for its pure release, have their place, but let's start with our best foot forward and give it our all, just like everything else in life.

"Gratitude," I muttered. "I apologize for throwing a pillow at you."

She shrugged. It was soft, at least. Let's see Dirty Dancing and now consume our fair share of chocolate ice cream.

"You're superior to this," I told myself. I picked up some toilet paper, wiped away the eyeliner that had gotten in my eyes, put my lipstick and mascara back on, and inhaled deeply twice.

It's time to show.

I glanced beyond the restroom door. Lee was already out the door, leaving my overnight bag on the ground.

Dickbag for fucking it.

I put my duffle bag and handbag onto the barstool behind me as I marched back onto the platform and grabbed the microphone.

As the words "Well folks, I just got dumped" seeped into my bones, a menacing snicker sprung from my throat. "Here's to scumbag lawyers and the girls who are stupid enough to fall in love with them," I said, raising my glass of water to the sky.

There was silence throughout the bar. The record player in the back just screeched to a stop, and I had the impression that I was in an old-fashioned movie. That terrible place, you could have heard a pin drop.

A muscular, bearded client yelled back from the bar, "To scumbags!" Thankfully, the others joined in.

I sat behind the little piano and let Say Something by A Great Big World stream out of my soul without skipping a beat.

The troubled singer spoke to the crowded pub, letting everyone know how she felt. On that platform, I felt like my heart was breaking with hers.

I had Jackie send her a drink on me after her set.

Jackie greeted her with a rock glass at the edge of the stage. Etta grinned while Jackie gestured to me.

As soon as the songbird fluttered to my side, my heart began to race. Her strapless, dark blue evening gown revealed her bare, exquisite shoulders as her long, dark hair was swept up in a bun. She sat beside me, the storm building in her irises meeting mine.

"Cheers," she said, chuckling as she shook hands with me.

"You were outstanding. After that performance, you deserved to have a drink purchased for you. I'm sorry to hear about the dishonest attorney.

She shrugged and threw a duffle bag at her feet. "I just shed a whopping 175 pounds of dead weight."

"I can sip on that."

"Are you someone I know?" She struggled to place me as her gaze swept over my face.

I said, "I come here a lot."

"Perhaps that's it then." Pulling at her hair, Etta let it flow in loose curls. Her black curls framed her face nicely, her beautiful green eyes dreamy.

Jackie pointed at my almost empty glass as she leaned over the bar. "Hayes, one more?"

Simply water. I have to go to the farm early and brightly.

"The barn?" Etta tilted her head to the side and questioned. "Where on earth is Manhattan's barn located?"

I defied the reality that I would reveal my true identity to the stunning songbird. "An ice rink is sometimes known as the barn. I had to leave in the morning to go skate.

"Are you not a little too big to be a figure skater?" Etta made fun of him.

I am undoubtedly too large and awkward to be a figure skater. My sport is hockey.

Like in a professional capacity? Are you well-known in any way?

Jackie set the water glass down in front of me and laughed.

"Cut it in half." Jackie turned aside as I glanced at her, covering her mouth to hide how much she was laughing.

"I play for the New York Otters, but I'm unsure if I would say I am famous." It prickled at the back of my neck.

"My name is Etta." She extended her hand to clap my hand.

"My name is Gret."

"That's not a name you hear very often."

"That's just a moniker."

"What does it stand for?"

I forcefully gulped. "You must swear not to laugh."

Etta grinned, holding up three fingers. "Honor of the scout, I refuse to laugh."

"Gretzky Hayes is my name." I detested my name, fuck it. Why couldn't my parents give me a typical name as they did for my two elder siblings? My sister got Gwen, and my brother got Garrett. And there I was, a man incapable of living up to the silliest first name imaginable.

"So you were forced to pursue a hockey career, then?" I observed Etta fending off fits of hysterics. "And I felt it was terrible that when I was three years old, my mom gave me the name Etta and threw me into voice lessons."

"I suppose our parents had great expectations for us. If nothing else, you are more than qualified to wear the shoes you were born into. When it comes to talent, I am at most middling.

"Go on, don't undervalue yourself."

You know, you didn't have a bad night alone. We can just end it there.

"So, your boyfriend brought you a bag containing a weekend's worth of stuff, told you that he already sublet the apartment, and dumped you in the middle of a set?"

"Fuck it. That is very terrible.

"Explain it to me." She rolled her eyes and took a sip of her amber beverage.

"My team lost the game a few hours ago."

"At least you have somewhere to stay this evening." Her voice broke a little as her gaze focused on the bar top.

A lightbulb went out at the most ridiculous thought I could have thought of. It was probably a combination of the alcohol and my debilitating desire to make amends for a terrible defeat.

Alright, this will be rather forward-thinking, but let's get started. Tonight, please accompany me home.

She shook her head, widening her gaze. "I have no idea who you are."

"Look, I'm not attempting to get in your pants or be creepy. In my residence, I have a spare room. I have an extra bed, so you have nowhere to go. As easy as that.

"Screw it." Etta swilled the remainder of her beverage. "It seems unlikely that I will be able to locate lodging in Manhattan at this late hour. Just swear that you won't skin suit me at all during the night.

How come? No fuck. How on earth could that possibly imply anything?

"You should watch more crime dramas," I said.

"Seemingly."

www.ingramcontent.com/pod-product-compliance
Lightning Source LLC
Chambersburg PA
CBHW052145110526
44591CB00012B/1870